The art of Feng Shui applied to your pets

Author: Gonzalo Estrada

Table of Contents

Content

Chapter 1: Understanding the Art of Feng Shui for Your Pets

The art of Feng Shui, as ancient as it is mysterious, has proven to have a significant impact on our lives and environments. But have you ever wondered how this ancient art can benefit your beloved pets? In this first chapter, we'll explore the basic principles of Feng Shui and how they can be beneficially applied to improve the well-being of your pets at home.

To better understand how Feng Shui can influence pets, we must first dive into its fundamentals. Feng Shui, which literally translates as "wind and water", seeks to balance the energies of a space to promote harmony and positive flow. It is based on the belief that everything in the universe is connected by a vital energy known as "Chi". By applying the principles of Feng Shui, we can harness and harmonize this energy, thus improving our emotional, mental and physical well-being.

So how does Feng Shui affect our beloved pets? As sensitive and highly intuitive beings, our pets are also influenced by the energies that surround them. If your environment is unbalanced or full of negative energies, this can affect your mood, behavior, and even your health. On the other hand, a space in harmony and balance can promote their well-being and happiness.

One of the most fundamental ways to apply Feng Shui for the benefit of your pets is to pay attention to the arrangement and organization of the furniture in your home. Animals, like humans, need to have a clear, open space to move and rest comfortably. Avoid excess furniture or objects that can block your path, creating a sense of claustrophobia or hindering your natural movement.

In addition, it is essential to consider the colors and textures we use in decorating our home. Just like us, our pets can be affected by the energy that emanates from different shades and materials. Opt for soft, relaxing tones in areas where they spend most of their time, avoiding colors that are too bright or aggressive. Choose natural and soft materials for your beds and places to rest, creating a cozy and comforting environment.

Another important aspect to consider is the location of the water features in your home. Water is a powerful symbol in Feng Shui and can influence the energy of your pets. If you have fish tanks or water fountains, make sure they are located in harmonious and balanced areas. Avoid placing them near their rest or eating area, as this can disturb their peace of mind.

Order and cleanliness also play a vital role in the well-being of your pets from a Feng Shui perspective. A messy space, with an accumulation of objects or dirt, can generate stagnant and dense energies that negatively affect your furry companion. He regularly spends time cleaning and keeping the space clean, thus promoting a lighter and more positive atmosphere.

As you gain more knowledge about the art of Feng Shui applied to your pets, you will realize that there are numerous ways to improve their well-being through the harmonization of their environment. In the second half of this chapter, we'll explore how Feng Shui can influence the choice of toys and accessories for your pets, as well as the creation of specific spaces to promote their relaxation and emotional balance. You'll discover how small changes can have a big impact on the lives of your beloved companions!

Read on and discover how you can apply the fascinating art of Feng Shui for the benefit and well-being of your adorable pets! The second half of this chapter will explore how Feng Shui can influence the choice of toys and accessories for your pets, as well as the creation of specific spaces to promote their relaxation and emotional balance. You'll discover how small changes can have a big impact on the lives of your beloved colleagues.

When choosing toys and accessories for your pets, it's important to consider their quality and material. Opt for toys that are made of safe and non-toxic materials, avoiding those that may be dangerous or contain components that are harmful to them. Also, make sure that the toys are appropriate for the size and age of your pets, as well as for their specific needs. By providing them with adequate toys, you will provide them with a healthy way to exercise and release energy, promoting their physical and mental well-being.

In addition, creating specific spaces for your pets in your home can be beneficial for their emotional balance. These spaces can be designated areas where they can rest, relax, or simply have a moment of calm. For example, you can create a cozy area with a soft and comfortable bed so they can rest, or a corner with pillows where they can lie down and enjoy a quiet moment. By providing them with their own place in your home, you will give them a sense of security and belonging, which will promote their emotional well-being.

In addition, it's important to consider the location of these specific spaces. Choose quiet areas away from the hustle and bustle or loud noises, so your pets can relax and unwind without unwanted distractions. Avoid placing these spaces near busy doors or windows, as the constant hustle and bustle can alter your peace of mind. By finding a suitable place for their moments of rest and calm, you'll be helping to balance their energy and providing them with a haven within your home.

Another aspect to consider is the importance of cleaning and organizing these spaces. Just as you benefit from a clean and tidy place, your pets can also feel more comfortable and balanced in a clean and tidy environment. Take regular time to clean and maintain these spaces, removing excess hair or dirt and making sure they are free of obstructions that may make it difficult for your pets to pass through. Remember that a clean and tidy space promotes a more harmonious and positive energy, which will benefit your adorable companions.

As you immerse yourself in the art of Feng Shui applied to your pets, you'll discover that there are numerous ways to improve their well-being and balance through small changes in their environment. From the location of the water features to the choice of the right toys and accessories, every detail can make a difference in the quality of life of your beloved companions. By understanding and applying the principles of Feng Shui, you will be creating a harmonious environment for your pets, promoting their happiness and well-being.

I hope this second half of the chapter has been useful for you to understand even more how the art of Feng Shui can benefit your pets. Continue to explore and learn about this fascinating art, and discover how small changes can have a big impact on the lives of your adorable companions. Feng Shui offers a holistic approach to improving the quality of life of our pets, promoting their physical, emotional and spiritual well-being.

Remember, every pet is unique and may have different needs and preferences. Observe and listen to your pets, so you can adapt the environment according to their specific needs. Applying Feng Shui to their spaces and carefully selecting the right toys and accessories are precious ways to show them how much you care about their well-being.

Continue to provide them with a harmonious and loving environment, and enjoy the benefits that the art of Feng Shui can bring to the lives of your beloved pets!

Chapter 2: The importance of balance in the environment

We will learn how to create a balanced and harmonious environment for our pets, promoting their well-being and health.

Pets are an important part of our lives. They provide us with companionship, unconditional love and joy, so it is essential to take care of them and provide them with an environment suitable for their physical and emotional development. Like us, pets are also affected by the environment in which they live, and this is where the art of Feng Shui takes center stage.

Feng Shui, an ancient oriental practice, consists of harmonizing spaces to achieve energy balance. This technique is based on the flow of energy, known as "chi", and seeks to optimize it to generate harmony and well-being. Applying Feng Shui principles to our pets' environment can help them find that much-needed balance.

The first step in creating a balanced environment for our pets is to pay attention to the distribution of space. A messy and chaotic environment can cause stress for animals, so it's important to keep a space clean and tidy. If there are too many objects or furniture in a room, our pets may feel overwhelmed and have difficulty moving freely.

In addition, it is essential to consider the location of objects within the space. According to Feng Shui, certain elements such as our pets' bed, their toys or their resting place, must be strategically placed to promote their well-being. For example, placing our pet's bed near a window will allow them to enjoy sunlight and fresh air, which will have a positive impact on their health and mood.

Another important aspect to consider is the use of colors in the environment. Colors influence our emotions and mood, and our pets can also be affected by them. For example, soft and harmonious tones such as green or blue can convey tranquility and calm, while bright, vivid colors can generate excitement. It is advisable to choose colors that adapt to the temperament of our pets to help them feel more balanced.

In addition to paying attention to the physical environment, it is essential to consider air quality and lighting in the space where our pets spend most of their time. An environment with good ventilation and adequate lighting will contribute to your overall well-being. Also, avoiding the presence of toxic substances or chemicals in your environment is crucial to avoid possible health problems.

In short, creating a balanced and harmonious environment for our pets is essential for their well-being and health. Applying Feng Shui principles can help us optimize the energy of the space and contribute to a fuller and happier life for our furry companions. In the second part of this chapter, we will explore how to use the influence of Feng Shui in the choice of decorative elements and how to adjust the space to facilitate its balance. Don't miss it! Once we have established the foundations for creating a balanced environment for our pets, it's time to delve into the choice of decorative elements and additional adjustments we can make to promote their well-being.

First of all, it is important to note that the decorative objects we choose can transmit different energies. Choose those that reflect calm and tranquility, avoiding those that can cause anxiety or stress in our pets. For example, images of animals in motion or with aggressive expressions can make them uncomfortable and alter their mood. Opt for paintings or photographs that reflect harmony and peace.

In addition, the materials of decorative objects also play an important role. Avoid those that are fragile or can cause harm to our pets. For example, glass objects that can break easily or ornaments with small parts that can be dangerous if ingested. Opt for strong and safe materials, such as natural woods or ceramics.

Another important consideration is the location of decorative objects. According to Feng Shui, there are specific places where certain objects can help balance the energy of our pets. For example, placing a water fountain in the north of the room can boost the energy of Water, which is associated with health and vitality. However, it is important not to clutter up the space with too many ornaments, as this can create a feeling of overwhelm in our pets.

In addition to the decorative elements, it is crucial to adjust the space to facilitate the balance of our pets. A proper distribution of furniture can positively influence your well-being. For example, make sure you leave enough space for them to move around comfortably and access their toys or feeders unhindered. Avoid placing furniture in places that obstruct their path or make them feel trapped.

It is also advisable to consider the specific needs of each type of pet. For example, cats need vertical scrapers to sharpen their nails and stretch. It seeks options that suit their preferences and provides multiple rest and play areas so that they can choose where to be at all times.

We must not forget the importance of cleaning and regular maintenance of the space in which our pets spend most of their time. Regularly cleaning your rest area, washing toys and brushing them frequently are actions that promote harmony and well-being. A pet in a clean and tidy environment will feel more comfortable and safe.

Finally, remember that every pet is unique and may have different preferences. Observe their behavior and reaction to the adjustments you make to their environment to make sure they feel comfortable and happy. If you notice any negative changes in their behavior, consider if there's anything you can change to improve their well-being.

In conclusion, Feng Shui applied to our pets provides us with tools to create a balanced and harmonious environment that favors their well-being and health. The right choice of decorative elements, the correct distribution of space and the regular care of their environment will help to make our pets feel comfortable and happy in their home. Let's give them the love and care they deserve, creating an environment that provides them with a full and happy life. See you soon!

Chapter 3: Choosing the Right Place for Your Pet

We will discover how to select the best place in our home so that our pets feel comfortable and in harmony.

It's well known that our homes are spaces full of energy, and this energy directly affects our pets. Like us, they need an environment where they can relax, play and rest in harmony.

Choosing the right place for your pet is critical to their emotional and physical well-being. By providing them with adequate space, we offer them the opportunity to fully develop and enjoy an optimal quality of life.

First, consider the size of your pet. If you have a large dog, it will need more space to move and run. Make sure the place you choose allows him to stretch and be comfortable. Consider having an outdoor area where you can play and sunbathe.

On the other hand, if you have a cat, you will know that sometimes they are very independent animals. However, they also need to feel safe and have their own place inside the house. You can create a corner in a quiet room with a soft bed and toys so they can relax and escape the hustle and bustle of home when they need to.

Another important aspect to consider is the ventilation of the place. Make sure the space intended for your pet is well ventilated, with access to a good stream of air. This will help prevent the accumulation of odors and ensure that they are constantly breathing fresh air.

Lighting also plays a crucial role in your pet's well-being. Just like us, they need natural light to stay healthy. If possible, choose a place where they can receive sunlight directly or, at least, indirectly. This will provide them with vitamin D and help them maintain a positive mood.

In addition, some animals, such as reptiles, require specialized lighting. Research your pet's specific needs and provide adequate lighting according to its species.

Now, let's talk about the strategic location within your home. It's important to consider that our pets seek to feel included in family life, so choose a place where they can interact with you and the rest of the family. For example, if you have a dog, it is advisable to locate their space near common areas of the house, such as the living room or kitchen.

Remember that every pet is unique and may have individual preferences. Observe their behavior and reactions to different spaces within your home. If you find that you are avoiding certain areas or showing discomfort, you may need to make adjustments to provide a more suitable and welcoming place.

In short, choosing the right place for our pets within our home is essential for their well-being. Consider their size, specific needs, lighting, ventilation, and strategic location. By providing them with a dedicated space adapted to their needs, we will be creating an environment where they can feel comfortable and in harmony.

In the second half of this chapter, we'll explore how to decorate your pet's space with feng shui elements to further enhance their well-being and balance. But for now, we'll let these initial recommendations settle in, and I invite you to continue discovering how you can help your pets find their ideal place in your home. Once you've chosen the right place for your pet, it's time to decorate it according to Feng Shui principles to further enhance their well-being and balance. Feng Shui is an ancient art that seeks to harmonize the energy of the environment to promote health and well-being, and you can also apply it to your pet's space.

One of the first things to consider is color. Colors play an important role in Feng Shui, as everyone has a different energy. For a calm and relaxing environment, choose soft, neutral colors, such as white, beige or light blue. Avoid bright or overly stimulating colors, as they can create stress for your pet.

In addition to color, you can also incorporate natural elements into your pet's space. Plants are a great way to introduce fresh, purifying energy. Choose plants that are non-toxic to your pets and place them strategically in the space. Not only will they give you a natural and beautiful touch, but they will also improve air quality.

Another aspect to consider is the organization. Keep your pet's space clean and tidy, avoiding clutter and excess objects. Clutter can hinder the circulation of energy and create a discordant environment. Make sure you have enough space for your pet to move around comfortably and that you provide them with a specific place for their toys and belongings.

Balance is another important Feng Shui principle. Try to make your pet's space symmetrical and balanced. Place the feeder and the drinker in opposite, equidistant places, and make sure that the toys are distributed harmoniously.

In addition to decorating, it is also essential to pay attention to the cleaning and maintenance of your pet's space. Keep the area clean and free of unpleasant odors, as this can affect your well-being. Clean food and water containers, as well as bed and toys regularly. This will not only improve your pet's hygiene, but it will also help to maintain positive energy in the space.

Remember that every pet is unique and may have individual preferences. Observe their behavior and their reactions to the changes you make in their space. If you notice that you avoid certain objects or colors, you may need to make adjustments to create a more welcoming and harmonious environment.

In short, applying Feng Shui principles to your pet's space can enhance their well-being and balance. Consider color, natural elements, organization, and balance when decorating your space. Pay attention to cleaning and maintenance, and look at your pet's individual preferences. By doing so, you'll be creating an environment where your pet will feel comfortable, in harmony and in sync with their environment.

As this chapter concludes, I invite you to continue exploring how to apply Feng Shui to other aspects of your pets' daily lives, such as their diet and daily routine. Remember that the well-being of your pets is essential to their happiness and health. Feng Shui can be a useful tool to help you create an environment conducive to your physical and emotional well-being. Keep learning and enjoying the company of your beloved pets in your harmonized home.

Chapter 4: The Power of Colors in Animal Welfare

We'll explore how colors can influence the mood and behavior of our pets, and how to select the right color palette to improve their well-being.

Our pets become beloved members of our family. They provide us with unconditional love, joy and constant companionship. For that reason, it's critical to create an environment that promotes their well-being and happiness. While we often focus on their diet and physical health, it's just as important to pay attention to their environment and how the colors that surround them can affect their mood and behavior.

Colors have a significant impact on our emotions and are present in all areas of our lives. Like us, pets are sensitive to visual stimuli and can experience changes in their mood depending on the colors that surround them. Understanding how colors influence our pets will allow us to create an optimal environment for their well-being.

The first step to harnessing the power of colors in the well-being of our pets is to know the emotional response that each of them can generate. Warm colors, such as red and yellow, tend to be stimulating and energetic. They can create a lively environment and encourage physical activity for our pets. On the other hand, cool colors, such as blue and green, have a more calming and relaxing effect. They can help reduce stress and create a sense of tranquility in our pets.

It is important to consider the individual characteristics of our pets when selecting the right color palette. Some animals may be more sensitive to certain colors than others. For example, cats have sharper vision in shades of blue and green, so they may be more attracted to colors in that range. Similarly, dogs may respond differently to colors depending on their breed and temperament.

But beyond individual preferences, we can use colors strategically to positively influence the behavior and mood of our pets. If we want to encourage relaxation and rest, we can use soft shades of blue or green in areas where our pets spend time to create a peaceful environment. On the other hand, if we want to promote activity and mental stimulation, we can incorporate bright, bright colors into the toys and accessories they use.

Choosing the right color palette is not only relevant for certain areas of our home, but also for the objects that our pets use on a daily basis. For example, your beds, blankets, food plates, and toys may have specific colors that influence your overall behavior and well-being. If we want our pets to feel safe and energetic, we can choose warm colors such as yellow or orange in their accessories. If, on the other hand, we want to promote calm and serenity, fresh shades of blue and green can be an excellent choice.

Some studies suggest that colors can also influence our pets' appetite and digestion. If we notice that our dog or cat shows little interest in their food, we could try using food plates in bright and vibrant colors to stimulate their appetite. However, it's important to remember that every animal is unique and may respond differently to these visual stimuli.

In short, colors have a real impact on the mood and behavior of our pets. By understanding how colors can influence them, we can select the right color palette to improve their well-being in all aspects of their lives. From decorating our home to the objects they use every day, colors play a fundamental role in the happiness and vitality of our beloved pets.

Now that we've explored how colors can influence our pets and how to select the right color palette, it's important to also consider using neutral colors in certain situations. While vibrant colors can be beneficial in some cases, too much visual stimulation can be overwhelming for our pets. That's why neutral tones such as white, gray and beige should also be taken into account.

These neutral colors create a calm and relaxing environment, especially in spaces where our pets rest and sleep. Providing them with a serene place to rest can help reduce stress and promote their overall well-being. In addition, neutral colors can be ideal for common areas where our pets interact with us and other family members. As they are more subtle tones, they will not generate excessive stimulation and will provide a balanced environment.

As we move forward in selecting colors for our pets, we must also consider contrast. Colors with high contrast can attract the attention and arouse the curiosity of our pets. For example, a blanket or toy with black and white striped patterns may be especially attractive to them. These types of visual stimuli can encourage their activity and play, keeping them entertained and mentally stimulated.

In addition to the color palette, we must also pay attention to the lighting in our pets' environment. Sunlight, for example, can have a positive effect on your well-being. Providing them with access to natural light can promote their vitality and emotional health. Colors can also interact with light in interesting ways: lighter, brighter tones can reflect more light, while darker tones can absorb it. In this way, we can strategically use colors in combination with lighting to create unique and attractive visual effects for our pets.

In conclusion, the power of colors in animal welfare is something that we should not overlook. Just as colors can affect our emotions and behavior, they can also influence our pets in significant ways. By creating a harmonious and balanced environment through a careful selection of colors, we can improve your quality of life and promote your well-being in all aspects.

By following these tips and taking into account the individual preferences of our pets, we can create a space that is pleasant and stimulating for them. Remember that selecting the right color palette is not only relevant for decorating our home, but also for the objects and accessories they use on a daily basis.

By understanding and applying the art of Feng Shui to our pets, we are showing how much we care about their well-being and happiness. Our pets deserve an environment that promotes their emotional balance and vitality, and colors are an invaluable tool to achieve this.

I hope you enjoyed this chapter on the power of colors in animal welfare. You now have the tools you need to apply Feng Shui to your pets and create an environment conducive to their happiness and vitality. In the next chapter, we'll explore how order and organization can influence the well-being of our pets. Don't miss it!

Chapter 5: Pet-friendly furniture and decor

We will discover how to choose suitable furniture and decorations for our furry friends, ensuring their comfort and safety at home. When we share our home with pets, it's essential to create an environment that fits their needs and provides them with a safe and welcoming space. In this chapter, we'll delve into the fascinating world of pet-friendly furniture and decor, providing tips and recommendations to help you make the best decisions for your four-legged companions.

One of the first things to consider when selecting furniture is durability. Pets, especially dogs and cats, tend to play, jump and scratch, so it's important to choose sturdy pieces that can withstand their daily activity. Opt for durable, easy-to-clean materials, such as waterproof or easy-care fabrics, such as leather or stain-resistant microfiber. These materials will make it easier to clean up hair and accidental spills, while minimizing the risk of damage and breakage.

In addition to durability, convenience is another crucial factor when selecting pet furniture. Consider ergonomics and the right size for your furry companion. Make sure that the sofas, beds, and chairs you choose are spacious enough for your pet to move and rest comfortably. Furniture with removable covers is also a great option, allowing you to wash it easily and maintain a clean, odor-free environment.

Design also plays an important role in pet-friendly furniture. Look for furniture with rounded corners and softened edges to avoid injuries and bumps. Avoid items that have small or loose items that could pose a choking hazard to your pet. In addition, choose stain-resistant color tones that fit the overall aesthetic of your home. This way, you can enjoy a harmonious and decorative space without sacrificing the comfort and safety of your furry friends.

Now, let's move on to pet-friendly decor. A wonderful way to provide a pleasant environment for our pets is to offer them their own and adapted spaces. For example, you can allocate a corner with a cozy bed and toys exclusively for them. This will give them a place to feel safe and relaxed, reducing their need to explore other places in the house that might be less suitable for them.

In addition, it is important to consider the type of decoration we choose. Avoid plants that are toxic to pets and place fragile or delicate objects out of reach of your furry friends. It incorporates attractive decorative elements for them, such as vertical scrapers for cats or interactive toys for dogs. These items will not only beautify your home, but they will also provide positive stimulus for your pets.

Remember that by choosing the right furniture and decor for your pets, you're creating an environment that promotes their well-being and happiness. Providing them with safe and comfortable spaces is an act of love and care for them. In the second half of this chapter, we'll explore more options and tips to make your home an ideal place for your beloved pets. Are you ready to discover the surprises that await us? Let's move forward together! In this second half of the chapter, we will continue to explore options and tips to make our home an ideal place for our beloved pets. Let's keep discovering more surprises together.

A key aspect to consider when choosing pet-friendly furniture and decor is safety. It's important to make sure that the objects in our home are not dangerous to our pets. For example, avoid small or fragile ornaments that could break and pose a risk of suffocation or injury. Also, make sure that the electrical cables are well protected and hidden to prevent your pets from nibbling on them and getting hurt.

Another way to provide a comfortable and safe environment for our pets is to adapt the furniture to their needs. Consider the height of the furniture and the access to it so that your pets can get on and off without difficulty. For example, if you have a cat, you can install high shelves or a scratch tower so that it has its own space in height. If you have small dogs, you can opt for raised beds that allow them to rest without being in direct contact with the cold floor.

In addition to furniture, the location of objects in our home is also important. It is advisable to avoid placing valuable or delicate objects near areas where our pets spend the most time, as they could accidentally knock them down or damage them. If you have cats, consider installing shelves or high spaces where they can climb and play, thus preventing them from climbing over furniture or curtains that could be damaged.

When it comes to decorating, it's important to remember that our pets also have sensory preferences and needs. For example, cats love scrapers and rough surfaces where they can sharpen their nails. Placing vertical scrapers in different areas of the house will provide them with an appropriate option to satisfy this natural instinct, while protecting our furniture.

For dogs, interactive toys are an excellent decorative option. These toys stimulate their minds and keep them busy, preventing them from getting bored and triggering unwanted behaviors, such as tearing down furniture or separation anxiety. You can find a wide variety of interactive toys, from prize dispensers to balls filled with food. Your dog will have fun and you can enjoy a wreck-free home!

Don't forget to consider the texture of the materials you choose for decoration. For example, cats enjoy soft, fluffy surfaces where they can rest and sharpen their claws. Placing comfortable rugs or blankets in places where they like to spend time will provide them with a cozy and pleasant space.

Finally, remember that every pet is unique and has its own preferences. Observe your furry companion and pay attention to what he likes and what he doesn't. Adjust the furniture and decor according to your individual needs and preferences.

In short, choosing pet-friendly furniture and decorations involves considering durability, comfort, and safety for our pets. In addition, we must adapt the environment to your individual sensory needs and preferences. Providing them with safe and comfortable spaces is one way to show them our love and care.

I hope you enjoyed this chapter and found useful tips to apply in your home! In the next chapter, we'll dive into the world of pet-friendly eating, exploring diet options and tips to keep our pets healthy and happy. Don't miss it!

Chapter 6: Energy Organization and Cleaning

We will learn organization and cleaning techniques that create a clean and balanced environment for our pets, promoting their well-being and happiness.

In our daily lives, we are often immersed in routine and give little importance to organizing and cleaning our home. However, when we share our space with pets, it's vital to keep in mind that their well-being and happiness are closely related to the environment in which they live.

The art of Feng Shui offers us a unique perspective to understand the influence that energy organization and cleaning have on the lives of our pets. We can apply their principles to harmonize the environment and create a positive and balanced space for them.

One of the fundamental techniques to achieve a healthy environment is to maintain cleanliness in our home. The energy accumulated in the mess and dirt can negatively affect our pets, causing stress and discomfort. Therefore, it is essential to establish regular cleaning routines to ensure greater harmony.

Cleanliness must go beyond physical appearance. To create effective energy cleaning, it is advisable to carry out "thorough" cleaning in all areas of the house. This involves getting rid of unnecessary objects, freeing up space and allowing energy to flow smoothly.

One way to do this is to start with our pets' bedroom. It's important to keep this space tidy and clean, as it's the place where they rest and recharge their energies. Removing any objects that are out of use and carefully selecting the toys and accessories they actually use, will provide them with a more serene environment conducive to their well-being.

Another area that requires special attention is the feeding area for our pets. This space must be kept clean and organized to ensure optimal nutrition and prevent the spread of germs. Regularly washing dishes and food and water containers, as well as keeping the area free of debris and dirt, will help create an environment in harmony with your health and vitality.

In addition to physical cleaning, it is important to pay attention to the organization of objects in the home. Clutter can block the flow of energy and create emotional imbalances in our pets. Keeping spaces free of obstacles and clutter can help them feel more secure and calm.

A useful technique is to use boxes or containers to organize our pets' toys and accessories. In this way, we not only prevent them from dispersing throughout the house, but we also provide them with a defined and tidy space, where they can find what they need without difficulty.

Energy organization and cleaning are fundamental aspects to consider in the well-being of our pets. By creating a clean and balanced environment, we give them the possibility to live in a harmonious place, where they can develop their energy in a positive way and achieve a greater degree of happiness.

In the next chapter, we'll explore other Feng Shui techniques that will allow us to maximize the well-being of our pets. We'll discover how the design and layout of spaces can influence their emotional and physical state. Don't miss it! The well-being of our pets is our highest concern as responsible owners. For this reason, in this chapter we are delving into Feng Shui techniques applied to our pets, focusing on energy organization and cleaning. As we have already mentioned, maintaining a clean and balanced environment is essential to promoting their well-being and happiness.

Continuing with our organization techniques, it is important to pay attention to our pets' resting spaces. A comfortable and quiet place to sleep goes a long way to your emotional and physical health. It is advisable to provide them with a suitable bed that fits their needs and preferences. The bed must be located in a place that provides them with privacy and tranquility, away from areas of high traffic or noise.

In addition, it is essential to keep bed linen and blankets clean and fresh. Washing these items regularly provides them with a pleasant, bacteria-free environment. Remember to use gentle, non-toxic cleaning products, as our pets are often sensitive to certain chemicals.

Continuing with the organization, it is also important to consider the places where our pets play and exercise. Just like humans, pets need to stay active and entertained to lead healthy lives. For this, it is essential to have a space dedicated to their games and physical activities.

Keep this space tidy and free of obstacles to avoid accidents and injuries. If you have toys or accessories that are no longer being used, it's a good idea to dispose of them responsibly. Remember that the stagnant energy generated by unnecessary objects can negatively affect our pets.

It's also important to choose carefully the toys we provide them. Choose those that are safe and appropriate for their species and size, avoiding those with toxic materials or small parts that can be ingested. Interactive toys and toys that promote environmental enrichment are great options for keeping our pets mentally stimulated.

Energy cleaning also requires attention to other aspects of the home. For example, it is important to keep windows and doors in good condition, as they are the energy inputs in our home. Make sure they are clean and functional, allowing natural light and fresh air to enter.

Also, pay attention to lighting in the home. Light plays an important role in the well-being of our pets, as it influences their mood and helps them to regulate their sleep and wake cycles. Use soft lights and avoid intense or flickering artificial lighting, as this can cause stress.

Finally, let's not forget that the balance between organization and energy cleaning depends not only on our home, but also on our own well-being. As owners, our pets can feel and reflect our emotions and energies. It is essential to take care of ourselves, practicing relaxation techniques and maintaining a positive attitude to transmit calm and balance to them.

In conclusion, applying Feng Shui principles to our pets involves maintaining a clean, organized and balanced environment in the home. Through physical and energetic cleansing, we can promote their well-being and happiness. Remember that the love and care we provide to our pets will be reflected in their quality of life. Don't hesitate to continue exploring the wonderful world of Feng Shui to maximize the well-being of your beloved pets.

I hope you enjoyed and found these organizing and energy cleaning tips useful for your pets. Soon, we will continue to explore additional Feng Shui techniques that will allow you to improve the quality of life of your pets. Keep learning and enjoying this wonderful philosophy!

Chapter 7: The Power of Sounds and Music

We'll explore how sounds and music can affect our pets' moods, and how to use them appropriately to create a calm and relaxing environment. Communication between humans and pets takes place in a variety of ways, and one of them is through sounds. Just like us, pets also experience emotions and react to different stimuli, and the sound world they find themselves in can have a significant impact on their well-being.

Sound is vibration, and our pets are extremely sensitive to the vibrations that surround them. A harmonious and soft sound can create calm and serenity in them, while a sudden or shrill noise can trigger their alert instinct and make them feel anxious or stressed. Music, in particular, has the ability to evoke emotions in our furry friends and can influence their behavior and mood.

When it comes to choosing the right music for your pets, it's important to consider their personality and individual preferences. Some dogs may enjoy soft, relaxing tunes, while others may prefer more lively rhythms. Likewise, cats may like classical or soft music, but they can each have their own preferences. Observing your pets' reactions while listening to different types of music is a great way to determine what they like and what they don't.

It's important to note that sounds and music can also be used to influence the behavior of our pets. For example, if you have an anxious or fearful dog, you can use relaxing music to help him calm down during stressful situations, such as a storm or a trip to the vet. In the same way, if you want to stimulate your pet during training, you can choose cheerful and energetic sounds that motivate them to participate and learn.

In addition to music, ambient sounds also play an important role in the lives of our pets. Constant and excessive noise can create a stressful environment and negatively affect your well-being. On the other hand, a calm and balanced sound environment can promote relaxation and rest. Trying to minimize loud noises and provide a peaceful environment at home can benefit the physical and emotional health of our pets.

It's crucial to remember that our pets also have different noise tolerance thresholds. Some may be more sensitive to certain sounds than others. Therefore, it is essential to be attentive to the reactions of our pets to different sound stimuli and to adjust the environment in which they live accordingly.

In the next chapter, we'll dive deeper into how to use sounds and music more specifically for the well-being of our pets. We'll explore different musical genres and ambient sounds that can be beneficial to them, providing practical tips to get the most out of this powerful tool. Get ready to discover how the right music and sounds can transform the lives of your beloved pets. Because the art of Feng Shui applied to them is much more than we imagine. Sounds and music can have a significant impact on our pets, and in this second part of the chapter, we'll dive deeper into how to use these effects in a specific way to promote their well-being.

One of the most common ways to use music to calm and relax our pets is through classical music. This genre usually has a calm rhythm and soft melodies that can have a calming effect on our furry friends. Some studies have shown that classical music can reduce stress levels in dogs, lowering their blood pressure and heart rate. Experiment with different pieces of classical music and see how your pet reacts. You may notice that some specific melodies have an even more relaxing effect on her.

In addition to classical music, there are also other musical genres that can influence the mood of our pets. For example, electronic music with energetic rhythms can make some dogs feel more active and playful, while soft, relaxing music can help cats relax and unwind. There's no one-size-fits-all answer for every pet, so it's important to look at each pet's individual reactions.

Not only should we consider the type of music our pets prefer, but also the way we play it. Some dogs and cats may benefit from speakers or headphones specially designed for pets, which can transmit sound more clearly and appropriately to their sensitive ears. It is also important to control the volume of the music, as a sound that is too loud can be annoying or stressful for our pets.

In addition to music, ambient sounds can also have an impact on the well-being of our pets. For example, the sound of nature, such as birds chirping or the rustling of leaves, can create a sense of peace and tranquility. On the other hand, loud and constant noises, such as traffic or household appliances, can create stress and anxiety in them.

To create a balanced sound environment, you can use pet sound devices that make relaxing sounds, such as waterfalls or soft rain. These sounds can help mask unwanted noises and create a peaceful environment for your pet.

It's important to remember that every pet is unique and may have different preferences and sound needs. Some pets may enjoy music and sounds at certain times of the day, while others may prefer silence. Watch your pet carefully and pay attention to their reactions and behavior to determine what types of sounds and music are best for them.

In short, sounds and music can have a significant impact on the mood and well-being of our pets. Experiment with different musical genres and sounds to discover what pleases them and what soothes them. Make sure you provide a balanced and calm sound environment to promote their physical and emotional health. Remember that the well-being of our pets is an important part of our home and using the art of Feng Shui applied to them can transform their lives in a positive way.

Chapter 8: Natural Elements in the Home

We will discover how to integrate natural elements into our home decor to improve the balance and connection of our pets with nature.

Home is a refuge for our pets, where they find tranquility, love and a space to be themselves. Like us, they are looking for an environment that provides them with harmony and well-being. That's why our home decor can influence their mood and behavior. In this chapter, we'll explore how to incorporate natural elements into our home to create a welcoming environment in tune with nature.

The choice of materials and colors in decoration can have a significant impact on our pets. Organic materials such as wood and wicker create a feeling of warmth and naturalness in the environment. The soft, rough textures stimulate our pets' senses, allowing them to interact pleasantly with their environment.

Colors also play a fundamental role in the atmosphere we create at home. The psychology of color teaches us that each shade has a different influence on our emotions and those of our pets. Earthy tones, such as olive green and brown, convey serenity and stability, while light tones, such as white and beige, provide luminosity and spaciousness. To achieve a balance in the decoration, it is advisable to combine different colors that complement each other and create a harmonious atmosphere.

Now, let's dive into the integration of plants in our home. Plants are natural elements that bring life and freshness to our spaces. In addition to being decorative, they also improve air quality by absorbing carbon dioxide and releasing oxygen. However, when choosing plants for our home, it's important to consider those that are safe for our pets. Some plants can be toxic if ingested, so we must inform ourselves beforehand about which are safe and which are not.

A safe and beneficial option for our four-legged friends is to incorporate aromatic herbs into pots. These will not only add a touch of freshness, but they can also benefit your health. Herbs such as peppermint, parsley and chamomile are known for their medicinal properties and can be consumed by pets in small quantities. Always check with your vet before offering them any plant, to make sure it fits their diet and doesn't cause them any problems.

By continuing to integrate natural elements, we cannot ignore the importance of natural light in the environment of our pets. Sunlight is essential for their well-being, as it provides them with vitamin D and stimulates the production of serotonin, known as the wellness hormone. Make sure your home has large windows that let in natural light during the day. Also, avoid obstructing windows with heavy curtains or furniture that limits the passage of light.

In conclusion, the integration of natural elements into our home decor is essential to improve the balance and connection of our pets with nature. Organic materials, the right colors, safe plants and natural light all contribute to creating a harmonious and enriching environment for our pets. In the second half of this chapter, we'll explore how to use water and other elements to further enhance this connection. Don't miss it!

Home is a special place for our pets, where they find love, comfort and a connection with the nature that surrounds them. In the first half of this chapter, we explored how integrating natural elements into decoration can improve the balance and well-being of our beloved pets. Now, let's dive even deeper into this connection and discover how to use water and other elements to enhance it.

Water is an essential element in the lives of our pets, as well as in ours. Providing them with an adequate space where they can drink, cool off and play is key to their well-being. An ideal option would be to install a pet water fountain in our home. These fountains provide fresh, filtered water, ensuring that our pets have access to clean water at all times. In addition, the soothing sound of flowing water can help create a relaxing and serene environment.

If your home has a garden or patio, consider including a pet pool. Pools not only provide them with a space to cool off on hot days, but they also allow them to exercise and have fun. Make sure that the pool has a ramp or ladder so they can get out easily and that it is always clean and safe for use.

Another element that we can incorporate into the decoration of our home are stones. Natural stones, such as quartz or jade, have energetic properties that can benefit both our pets and ourselves. Placing stones in strategic places in the house, such as near our pets' beds or in the corners where they spend the most time, can create a sense of calm and balance.

In addition to stones, we can also use seashells to decorate. Not only do shells add a maritime touch to our decor, they can also remind our pets of the tranquility and freedom of the ocean. Place shells in decorative vases or plates where our pets can safely observe and explore them.

Another natural element that we cannot ignore is fresh air. Ventilating our home is essential to ensure that our pets breathe clean and healthy air. Open windows regularly and use air purifiers to remove potential allergens or harmful particles. A well-ventilated room with adequate air circulation can improve the health and well-being of our pets.

Last but not least, is the importance of creating outdoor spaces for our pets. If you have a garden or yard, make sure it's safe and free from hazards. It provides shaded areas where they can rest and play, and places toys and natural elements such as logs or branches to stimulate their sense of exploration and play.

In conclusion, integrating natural elements into our home decor can greatly benefit our pets. Incorporating water, stones, seashells and fresh air into your environment will contribute to creating a harmonious environment in tune with nature. In addition, ensuring that they have access to safe outdoor spaces will allow them to enjoy the beauty and freedom of the outside world. Always remember to take into account the specific needs of your pet and adapt the decoration according to their preferences. Our pets deserve a home full of love, harmony and connection with nature!

Chapter 9: Rest and Comfort Zones

We will learn how to create comfortable and cozy resting spaces for our pets, promoting their well-being and providing them with a safe place to relax.

Our pets also need their own space for relaxation and comfort. Just like us humans, animals need a quiet and welcoming place where they can rest and feel safe. In this chapter, we'll explore how to create these rest areas for our beloved pets, allowing them to enjoy moments of relaxation and comfort.

When we talk about rest areas, we don't just refer to a simple bed or a random corner in our house. We are referring to a space designed especially for them, designed with love and care, that reflects their personality and meets their needs. By providing them with an adequate place to rest, we will be contributing to their physical and emotional well-being.

First of all, it is essential to consider the individual preferences of our pets. Some animals prefer to be close to us, while others need a farther away place to feel safe. Watch your pet closely and learn to understand its signs. Do you prefer to look for cool or warm places? Do you like being at heights or do you find it more comfortable in lower places?

Once you understand your pet's preferences, you can create the perfect rest area for them. You can start by selecting a quiet space in your home where there isn't a lot of traffic or noise. Avoid placing it near electronic devices or sources of noise that could scare or disturb it. It is also important to ensure that the area is free from hazards to avoid accidents.

Then, choose a comfortable bed or mat for your pet. You can find a variety of options on the market, from soft beds to orthopedic mats, depending on your pet's specific needs. Make sure the size is right so you can stretch and move freely.

To make this seating area an even more welcoming place, consider adding items that provide safety and comfort. You can place a soft, warm blanket for him to cuddle up in, or maybe a favorite toy to provide him with entertainment and company. Always remember to keep the objects you place in the rest area clean, as hygiene is essential for their well-being.

In addition, it's important to ensure that your pet has access to fresh water and food near their rest area. This will allow you to cover your basic needs without having to travel far from your place of comfort. Place a clean bowl of water and food and always keep them stocked.

Remember that your pets' needs can change over time, so it's important to regularly assess whether their rest area is still comfortable and satisfying for them. Observe their behavior and if you notice any signs of discomfort or stress, make any necessary adjustments.

Creating a suitable resting space for our pets is a tangible way of showing them our love and care. By providing them with a safe and comfortable place, we give them the opportunity to rest and recharge, thus contributing to their overall well-being.

In the next chapter, we will explore design and decoration techniques that will help us optimize these rest areas and turn them into even more welcoming spaces for our beloved pets. Don't miss it!

Once you've created the perfect space for your pet, it's important to pay attention to their behavior and make sure they feel comfortable and safe in their rest area. See if your pet spends a lot of time in their relaxation corner or if they prefer to find other places to rest. If you notice that you are avoiding your rest zone or showing signs of stress, you may need to make some adjustments.

One way to make the space even more inviting is to add items that stimulate your pet's senses. For example, you can incorporate relaxing scents, such as lavender or chamomile, using essential oils. You can also place some interactive toys to keep your pet entertained and mentally stimulated. Remember to rotate these toys regularly to avoid getting bored with them.

In addition, don't forget that Feng Shui also plays an important role in the rest areas of our pets. Try to keep the space tidy and free of clutter, as this will contribute to a sense of calm and tranquility. Avoid placing sharp or glass objects near your rest area, as they could pose a danger.

Another aspect to consider is the location of the rest area. Depending on your pet's preferences, you can choose a spot near a window so they can enjoy natural light and observe the outside. You can also consider placing your bed near a heat source in winter, to provide you with a feeling of warmth and comfort.

Remember that every pet is unique and their needs may vary. Some pets may prefer higher places, such as shelves or shelves, while others may feel safer in lower, more sheltered places. Watch and listen to your pet to adapt their resting space to their individual preferences.

Sometimes, you may need to make changes to the design of your pet's rest area to adapt it to their growth or changes in their health. For example, if your pet develops mobility problems or arthritis, they may need a more padded or better-supported orthopedic bed to ease any discomfort. By keeping attentive to the changing needs of our pets, we provide them with greater well-being and comfort.

In addition to creating an adequate rest area, it's important to establish a rest routine for your pet. Try to set regular sleep and wake times so that your pet can have a structure and adapt to a healthy sleep pattern. This will help you feel more balanced and have a greater sense of security.

In conclusion, creating a comfortable and welcoming rest area for our pets is essential for their overall well-being. By understanding their individual preferences and providing them with a space designed with love and care, we are contributing to their physical and emotional comfort. Remember to observe your pet's behavior and make the necessary adjustments to ensure that their rest area is a safe and pleasant place. Your pet will thank you with their unconditional love and companionship!

I hope you enjoyed this chapter about rest and comfort zones for our beloved pets! In the next chapter, we will continue to explore design and decoration techniques that will help us optimize these rest areas and turn them into even more welcoming spaces. Don't miss it!

Chapter 10: Play Spaces
and Physical Activity

We will explore how to design stimulating and safe play areas for our pets, promoting their physical and mental health.

When we share our lives with a pet, it's important to provide them with an environment where they can play and exercise properly. Play and physical activity are fundamental to the well-being of our beloved pets, as they allow them to release accumulated energy, stay in shape and stimulate their minds.

The first step in designing a suitable play space is to assess the size and needs of our pet. If we have an active and energetic dog, it is advisable to have a large space where he can run freely. This can be a fenced backyard, a dog park, or even a spacious room inside our home.

It is important to ensure that the play area is free of dangerous objects or that may pose a risk to our pet. Removing broken toys, loose wires, or toxic plants can prevent unnecessary accidents. In addition, let's make sure that the space is clean and clear to avoid obstructions that could interfere with our pet's play.

Once we have created a safe environment, it's time to provide suitable toys and play items for our pet. Interactive toys, such as feeding puzzles, are ideal for stimulating the minds of our furry friends while they play. We can also incorporate natural elements, such as tree trunks or scalable structures, to create an enriching gaming environment.

If we have cats, the addition of scratching posts and elevated places, such as shelves or rest stations at height, will provide them with options to climb and exercise their hunting skills. Toys that mimic prey, such as feathers or balls, can be especially attractive to them.

In addition to toys, it's important to spend time playing with our pets interactively. This will not only strengthen our bond with them, but it will also provide them with the physical and mental stimulation they need. We can use balls, ropes or even search games to encourage their activity and promote their well-being.

Another key factor for designing play spaces is the choice of materials. Let's opt for surfaces that are friendly to our pets' paws, avoiding those that could cause them damage or slips. Some recommended options are artificial grass, sturdy carpets or wooden floors with a non-slip finish.

Once we have designed a stimulating and safe play space for our pet, it is essential to incorporate it progressively into their daily routine. Encouraging their regular use and providing them with access to this space on a consistent basis will encourage their gaming instinct and help keep them active and happy.

In conclusion, the design of play and physical activity spaces is essential to promote the well-being of our pets. Providing a safe environment, providing suitable toys and spending time playing interactively are fundamental actions to keep our pets physically active and mentally stimulated. In the second part of this chapter, we'll explore additional techniques and considerations to ensure maximum fun and physical activity for our beloved pets. Let's continue our journey together in the next part of this fascinating chapter! In this second part of the chapter, we will continue to explore more techniques and considerations to create ideal play and physical activity spaces for our pets. In addition to providing them with a safe environment and providing them with suitable toys, there are other ways to keep our furry friends active and happy.

An interesting option is the presentation of prizes during the game. We can use healthy and delicious snacks as a reward when our pet performs some desired behavior during the game. This not only stimulates their mind and learning abilities, but it also strengthens the bond between us and our loyal friends.

Another fun strategy is to create game circuits in designated spaces. We can use furniture, boxes or tunnels to create an interesting route where our pets can run, jump and explore. This gives them a physical and mental challenge, while encouraging their curiosity and keeping them busy.

In addition, it is important to adapt the play space according to the specific needs of each pet. For example, if we have a small breed dog, we may need a play space inside our home. We can use play mats or a padded area with interactive toys to provide them with physical and mental stimulation without taking up much space.

For those who have fish or turtles as pets, it is also possible to design suitable play areas for them. We can add decorative elements to their aquariums, such as rocks, caves or aquatic plants, that provide them with opportunities to explore and hide. Remember that, even if we don't interact directly with these animals as we do with dogs or cats, they also need an enriching environment for their well-being.

As for cats, it is important to offer them different play options. We can rotate toys regularly to keep you interested and provide variety in your daily routine. Vertical scrapers, hanging toys and tunnels are great options for keeping our cats active and stimulated.

It is also essential to remember that, when designing play spaces for our pets, we must consider safety both for them and for ourselves. Let's avoid using small, loose objects that could pose a suffocation hazard for them. We must also ensure that play areas are free of toxic substances or chemicals that may be harmful to your health.

Finally, we can't forget that playing time and physical activity is also an ideal time to strengthen our bond with our pets. Let's spend time interacting with them, encouraging interactive play and affectionate communication. This not only gives them the physical and mental stimulation they need, but it also makes them feel loved and valued.

In conclusion, creating stimulating and safe play and physical activity spaces is essential to promote the well-being of our pets. By adapting the space to their specific needs, offering them suitable toys and spending time playing interactively, we are providing our furry friends with a way to release accumulated energy, stay fit and stimulate their minds. By following these guidelines, we can ensure that our pets are physically active and mentally happy.

Thank you for joining us in this fascinating chapter!

Chapter 11: Pet-friendly plants and gardens

Plants and gardens can provide a stimulating and harmonious environment for our pets. Not only do they beautify our home, but they can also support your physical and mental well-being. However, it is essential to note that not all plants are safe for our beloved pets. In this chapter, we'll discover which plants are suitable and how we can create a pet-friendly garden that provides a safe space for our furry friends.

Nature and the green environment can have a positive effect on the health of our pets. The presence of plants in our home or garden can help reduce stress, improve mood and stimulate your senses. However, some plants can be toxic and pose a danger to our four-legged friends.

Some common plants that we should avoid including in our pet-friendly garden are: the lily, the azalea, the sword fern, aloe vera and English ivy. These plants can cause serious health problems if ingested or even if animals come into contact with their sap. To avoid possible poisoning, it is essential to inform ourselves about the plants we have and to ensure that they are safe for our pets.

On the other hand, there are numerous plants that are safe and pose no threat to our pets. Some examples include the bamboo palm, African violet, catnip, rose, daisy, and croton. These plants can be part of our pet-friendly garden, providing our furry friends with a pleasant and stimulating environment.

When creating a pet-friendly garden, it's crucial to consider the specific needs of our pets. For example, if we have an active dog that enjoys running and playing outside, we must ensure that we have enough space for him to move freely. In addition, it is important to have shaded areas where they can rest and shelter from the sun.

It is also advisable to incorporate interactive elements into our garden, such as pet toys or water fountains. These elements can help keep our furry friends entertained and stimulated, promoting their well-being and preventing destructive behaviors due to boredom.

In addition, it is important to consider the size and structure of our plants, especially if we have cats. Cats are known for climbing and exploring, so it's essential to avoid climbing plants or shrubs that could pose a safety hazard.

In short, creating a pet-friendly garden requires a careful selection of plants and a consideration of the needs of our pets. We must always ensure that the plants we include are safe and do not pose a risk to your health. Remember, the most important thing is to provide a stimulating and safe environment for our furry friends. Now that we know which plants are safe for them, it's time to explore how we can incorporate them into our garden. In the second half of this chapter, we will learn about landscape design and how to create a harmonious space that promotes the happiness of our pets. We invite you to continue this exciting adventure together! When creating a pet-friendly garden, we must not only consider the right plants, but also the design and layout of our outdoor space. The arrangement of plants and items in the garden can have a significant impact on the well-being of our pets. Next, we'll explore some recommendations for designing a harmonious space that promotes the happiness of our furry friends.

First of all, it's important to consider the individual needs of our pets. For example, if we have a cat, it may need elevated areas to climb and observe its environment. We can incorporate furniture or structures for cats that provide them with height opportunities, such as climbing towers or shelves on the wall. These elements will not only satisfy their natural need to climb, but they will also allow them to have a panoramic view of their territory.

For dogs, it's essential to have open spaces where they can run and play. We can delimit specific areas, such as a play area or an exercise track, using fences or elements that mark the limits. In addition, we can incorporate obstacles or interactive toys that stimulate their physical and mental activity.

As for rest areas, it is essential to provide areas that are covered and protected from the sun and rain. They can be structures such as booths or simply shaded areas with the help of trees or umbrellas. These spaces will provide our pets with a safe place where they can rest and shelter at any time of the day.

In addition to specific areas for our pets, it's also important to consider the function and style of the garden as a whole. Balance and harmony are key elements of Feng Shui, so we must ensure that our garden has a pleasant layout and aesthetics.

We can achieve this by using a combination of plants of different heights, sizes, and colors. For example, we can opt for hanging potted plants to add dimension at higher levels, leafy shrubs to create visual barriers, and colorful flowers to add a touch of joy. Using items such as rocks, stones, or fountains can also add an element of tranquility and serenity to the garden.

In addition, it is advisable to avoid excessive decorative elements or furniture that can obstruct the movement spaces of our pets. It's important to allow them to have the freedom to explore and move unhindered in their environment.

Finally, it is essential to keep our garden in good shape and free of unwanted or toxic plants. We must perform regular maintenance, pruning plants properly and eliminating weeds. It's also important to avoid using toxic chemicals, such as pesticides or fertilizers, that can pose a danger to our pets.

In short, designing a pet-friendly garden involves considering the needs of our pets, while creating a harmonious and aesthetically pleasing space. By providing areas for play, rest and exploration, as well as a careful selection of plants and a balanced distribution, we will be creating an environment that will promote the physical and mental well-being of our furry friends.

I hope you enjoyed this chapter on pet-friendly plants and gardens. Now you have the tools you need to create a stimulating and safe space for your pet. In the next chapter, we'll explore how to apply Feng Shui principles to the interior of our home, to create a harmonious environment that benefits both our pets and ourselves. I invite you to continue this exciting adventure together!

Chapter 12: Feng Shui to harmonize the relationship with other pets

We will learn how to apply Feng Shui to improve coexistence and harmonize the relationship between several pets in our home.

The relationship between pets living in the same space can be a challenge for many pet owners. No matter how much love and care we give them, sometimes our beloved pets can conflict with each other. However, with the wisdom of Feng Shui, we can find the balance and harmony necessary so that all the furry members of our household can peacefully coexist.

First, it's important to understand that every pet has their own unique personality and energy. As owners, we must be attentive to these characteristics and respect the individual needs of each animal. Feng Shui teaches us that we must create balanced and harmonious spaces for our pets, allowing them to express themselves and relate in harmony.

A fundamental aspect of Feng Shui to harmonize the relationship between several pets is the adequate space and distribution of resources. Each pet must have its own place to rest, feed and play. These spaces, preferably, should be separated to avoid any sense of competition or territoriality. In addition, it is essential to have enough toys, scrapers and other fun items to help keep our pets entertained and satisfied.

Another aspect to consider is cleanliness and order in the home. Clutter and the accumulation of objects can generate energy instability, affecting the mood of our pets. Feng Shui recommends keeping a space clean and organized, ensuring that every corner is free from obstructions and clutter. This will provide a sense of calm and serenity that will favor peaceful coexistence among our beloved pets.

In addition to the physical environment, it's important to pay attention to the energy that we ourselves emit as pet owners. Our own emotions and attitudes can influence the behavior of our animals. Feng Shui invites us to cultivate positive and calm energy, transmitting love, balance and respect to our pets. By doing so, we will be creating a harmonious environment conducive to a peaceful relationship between them.

To harmonize the relationship between several pets in our home, it is also essential to observe their body language and behavior. Feng Shui teaches us to interpret the signals that our pets send us through their posture, gestures and facial expressions. By understanding their non-verbal communication, we can identify tense situations and act early to prevent conflicts. In addition, Feng Shui gives us guidelines for balancing the elements in space, placing objects or colors that promote peace and harmony.

Remember that every pet is unique and may require different techniques to improve relationships with other pets in the home. Watch and listen to your beloved pets, give them the love, attention and space they need. With patience and knowledge of Feng Shui, you will be able to create an enriching environment where all your pets can live in peace and happiness.

This concludes the first part of this chapter on Feng Shui applied to the harmonization of the relationship between several pets in our home. In the second part, we'll explore additional techniques and tips to strengthen the bonds between our furry friends. Arouse curiosity and emotion in your pets, they will be eager to discover how to further enhance peaceful coexistence in their home! In this second part of the chapter, we will continue to explore additional techniques and tips to strengthen the bonds between our beloved pets and achieve peaceful coexistence in our home.

One of the keys to harmonizing the relationship between several pets is proper socialization. When introducing a new pet into the home, it's important to do so gradually and in a controlled manner. Feng Shui teaches us that we must allow pets to get to know each other in a neutral environment, avoiding any sense of territorial invasion. This may involve holding meetings in a park or in an outdoor space where both pets feel comfortable and relaxed.

During the first few interactions, it's essential to be present and observe the behavior of pets. Pay attention to their body language and be sure to intervene if you notice signs of tension or aggression. Feng Shui reminds us that it is important to transmit peaceful and balanced energy through our presence and attitude. By doing so, we will be providing our pets with a safe and harmonious environment so that they can relate in a positive way.

Another aspect to consider is the mental and physical stimulation of our pets. Feng Shui suggests that we create an enriching environment for them, providing toys and activities that keep them busy and stimulated. For example, you can use interactive toys that require skill and skills to solve a problem. In this way, you'll be encouraging cooperative play between your pets and strengthening their relationship.

In addition, it is important to establish routines and schedules for our pets. Feng Shui teaches us that animals feel more secure and balanced when they have a clear structure and limits in their daily lives. Establishing feeding schedules, walks and moments of play will help create a predictable and stable environment, which is essential for a harmonious coexistence between several pets.

Relaxation and peace are essential elements for Feng Shui. By providing our pets with quiet and safe spaces, we are allowing them to calm down and find their emotional balance. This may involve creating separate rest areas for each pet, where they can retire and relax when they need to. You can also use the massage or aromatherapy technique to promote relaxation and well-being in your pets.

It's also important to pay attention to possible energy imbalances in the home that could affect the relationship between pets. Feng Shui teaches us that natural elements such as plants and water fountains can help balance energy in a space. You can place plants in different areas of the house or install a water feature to create a harmonious and peaceful environment for all your pets.

Finally, remember that each pet is a unique and special being, with its own needs and personality. Patience and love are essential for cultivating a harmonious relationship between them. Feng Shui invites us to be aware of our own emotions and attitudes towards our pets, always transmitting love, respect and balance to them.

With these additional techniques and tips, you'll be on your way to strengthening the bonds between your pets and creating a harmonious home. The key is to observe, listen and adapt Feng Shui practices to the individual needs of each pet. Remember that balance and harmony are possible, and with love and patience, you will ensure that all your pets coexist in peace and happiness.

This concludes this chapter on Feng Shui applied to harmonizing the relationship between several pets in our home. I hope these tips and techniques will help you create a nurturing environment for your beloved pets. Enjoy the wonderful coexistence with your furry friends following the principles of Feng Shui!

Chapter 13: The Influence of Feng Shui on Animal Behavior

We'll explore how the art of Feng Shui can influence the behavior of our pets and how to use it to promote balanced behavior.

Since ancient times, Feng Shui has been used to harmonize spaces and promote people's well-being. However, its application is not limited only to humans, as it can also have a significant impact on the behavior of our beloved pets.

Our pets are a fundamental part of our lives, providing us with unconditional love and companionship. But, just like us, they can also be affected by the environment in which they live. That's why, by applying Feng Shui principles to our homes, we can help our pets find the balance and harmony they need.

One of Feng Shui's main influences on animal behavior is through the organization and arrangement of space. By creating a tidy and unobstructed environment, we allow energy to flow properly, which is vitally important for both people and pets.

It's critical to ensure that there's enough space for our pets to move freely and feel comfortable. We must avoid having unnecessary furniture or objects that could limit their mobility. In the same way, it is important that rest and play areas are well defined, so that our pets can find their own space and carry out their activities properly.

Another aspect to consider is the choice of colors and materials in the decoration of our home. Feng Shui teaches us that every color and material has a unique energy that can influence our mood and well-being. The same goes for our pets. It is important to consider the colors that give them peace and calm, and to use them in items such as beds, toys or even on the walls of their rest areas.

In addition, it is essential to pay attention to the location of items and objects within our home. For example, placing our pet's bed in a position that allows them to have a clear view of the front door can give them a sense of security and control over their environment. Also, we must avoid placing the bed or toys near windows or doors that generate drafts, which can cause stress or discomfort.

Balanced lighting also plays a fundamental role in the well-being of our pets. Just like us, they need natural light to maintain a healthy and energetic mood. Therefore, it's important to ensure that they have access to well-lit areas during the day, and to provide them with a soft, relaxing light during the night to promote adequate rest.

In short, the art of Feng Shui can be a powerful tool to improve the behavior and well-being of our beloved pets. By applying their principles to our home, we are creating an environment in which energy flows in a harmonious and balanced way, which has a positive impact on the behavior of our faithful companions.

In the second part of this chapter, we'll explore in greater depth how to use Feng Shui objects and symbols to influence the behavior of our pets, as well as practical tips for maintaining a strong and healthy connection with them. Are you ready to discover the secrets of Feng Shui applied to your pets? Keep reading in the second part of this fascinating chapter. In the second part of this chapter, we will delve into how we can use the art of Feng Shui to positively influence the behavior of our beloved pets. In addition, I will also provide practical tips for maintaining a strong and healthy connection with our faithful companions.

One of the first ways that Feng Shui can influence animal behavior is through the proper selection of objects and symbols. Some objects such as water fountains can help create a relaxing and harmonious environment for our pets. The sound of flowing water can have a calming effect on them, which can reduce stress and anxiety. In addition, water fountains can also help keep our pets hydrated and promote their overall well-being.

Feng Shui symbols can also have a significant impact on the behavior of our pets. For example, using protective symbols, such as Chinese characters for good luck or Feng Shui charms, can help create a safe and positive environment for our pets. In addition, symbols that represent good health and longevity can help promote healthy living for our dear companions.

In addition to using objects and symbols, it is also important to establish routines and maintain clear communication with our pets. Pets are very sensitive to changes in their daily routine and to the energy we transmit to them. Therefore, it is essential to establish fixed times to feed them, take them out for a walk and play with them. This will provide them with security and stability, which will be reflected in their balanced and happy behavior.

Communication also plays a key role in connecting with our pets. We must learn to read their signs and respond to their needs in an empathetic way. Observing their body language, paying attention to their facial expressions and tone of voice will help us to better understand their emotions and moods. In addition, the language of touch is also crucial. Caressing them gently and providing them with relaxing massages will help them release tension and strengthen our emotional bond.

In addition, Feng Shui teaches us to be aware of our own energy and how it affects our pets. Our animals are sensitive to our moods and emotions. If we're stressed or anxious, they probably are, too. Therefore, it's important to take care of our own energy and look for ways to stay balanced and in harmony. Meditation, the practice of yoga or any activity that allows us to relax and release tension will be beneficial both for us and for our pets.

In short, the art of Feng Shui can positively influence the behavior and well-being of our pets. By carefully selecting objects and symbols, establishing routines, maintaining clear communication, and caring for our own energy, we can create an environment where our pets feel safe, balanced, and loved. Remember that our pets are part of our family and depend on us for their happiness and well-being. By following the principles of Feng Shui, we will be cultivating a space where our pets can flourish and live a full life with us.

I hope this chapter has been useful to you and that you find inspiration in the art of Feng Shui to improve your relationship with your pets. In the following chapters, we'll explore more ways to apply Feng Shui to the lives of our beloved companions and provide practical advice on how to maintain a strong and healthy connection with them. Don't miss it!

Remember that each animal is unique and can respond differently to Feng Shui techniques, so it's always important to watch and listen to our pets to adapt our practices to their individual needs.

Chapter 14: The Art of Feng Shui in Animal Training

We will discover how to use Feng Shui principles to improve the training process for our pets, promoting a harmonious and effective relationship.

Training our beloved pets can be a challenge, but with the right approach and application of Feng Shui principles, we can significantly improve this process. Feng Shui is an ancient Chinese art that seeks to harmonize the energy of a space and, by applying it to animal training, we can create a positive and balanced environment that facilitates communication and learning.

To begin with, it's essential to understand that our pets are sensitive to the energy of their environment. By applying the principles of Feng Shui, we can create a space that promotes calm, concentration and confidence in our animals, allowing them to learn and adapt effectively.

The first step is to evaluate the layout of the space where we will carry out the training. Feng Shui teaches us the importance of organization and cleanliness in our environment. A messy or dirty space causes energy imbalances that can distract and generate anxiety in our pets. Keeping the training area tidy, free of unnecessary objects and in a state of proper cleanliness, will help create an environment conducive to learning.

Another crucial aspect is the choice of colors. Feng Shui believes that colors have a direct influence on our energy and emotions, and this also applies to our pets. By selecting colors that convey calm and balance, such as soft shades of blue or green, we will be providing our animals with a calm atmosphere that will help them concentrate and relax during training.

In addition to colors, lighting also plays an important role. Natural light is preferable, but when this is not possible, it is advisable to use soft, diffused lighting. Let's avoid intense and direct light, as it can cause tension and stress in our pets. A pleasant light environment will help create a sense of harmony and well-being during training sessions.

The arrangement of furniture and objects in space is also essential for applying Feng Shui in training. We must ensure that there are no obstacles or furniture that hinder the movement of our pets. A large and unobstructed space will allow them to move freely and comfortably, facilitating the learning process.

In addition to the physical organization of space, we must pay attention to energy in motion, known as Chi. Chi must flow smoothly and unobstructed in the training area. To achieve this, we can use elements such as water fountains or fans to help activate and move energy. This will create a stimulating environment that is conducive to learning for our pets.

In short, by applying Feng Shui principles to the training of our pets, we create an energetically balanced environment that promotes concentration, calm and effective communication. From the organization and cleanliness of the space, to the choice of appropriate colors and the arrangement of the furniture, every detail helps to establish an atmosphere conducive to learning.

In the second half of this chapter, we will explore how to use natural elements and other aspects of Feng Shui to further enhance the training of our pets. Keep an eye out for the continuation of these techniques that are sure to surprise you and help you in your relationship with your beloved animal companion. Harmony is within our reach, and Feng Shui accompanies us on this exciting journey towards a deeper and richer relationship with our pets. In the second half of this chapter, we will continue to explore how to use natural elements and other aspects of Feng Shui to further enhance the training of our pets. We will continue to discover techniques and practical advice that will help us establish a deeper and more enriching relationship with our beloved animal companions.

One of the key recommendations of Feng Shui applied to animal training is the use of natural elements to improve the energy of the space. Plants, for example, can be excellent allies, since they not only add beauty and freshness to the environment, but they also purify the air and generate a harmonious flow of energy. Choose plants suitable for the training space, such as bamboo or lavender, that transmit calm and serenity, and place them strategically to balance the energy of the room.

Another important aspect is the use of aromatherapy to create a relaxing and stimulating environment for our pets. Essential oils, such as lavender or jasmine, can help calm anxiety and promote concentration during training sessions. Add a few droplets to an aroma diffuser or mix with water in a spray to spray the environment. Remember that animals have a more developed sense of smell than ours, so it's important to use safe and properly diluted essential oils.

Feng Shui also teaches us about the importance of balancing the five elements in space. These elements are wood, fire, earth, metal and water, and each represents a specific energy. We can incorporate these elements through decorative objects or accessories to stimulate different aspects of our pets' learning. For example, a water source would represent the water element, promoting fluidity and adaptability. Meanwhile, candles could represent the fire element, providing warm and stimulating energy.

In addition to these elements, it is essential to establish a coherent and consistent training routine for our pets. Feng Shui teaches us that regularity and consistency create a sense of stability and security in the environment. This also applies to animal training. Establishing specific times and spaces for training sessions will help our pets understand and adapt to the learning process more effectively.

We cannot forget the importance of non-verbal communication during training. Our pets are very sensitive to our emotions and body expressions. We must maintain a calm, serene and positive attitude during the sessions to give them confidence and motivation. Feng Shui reminds us that our energy is reflected in the environment, so we must be aware of our mood and keep it in harmony during the training process.

Finally, let's remember that every pet is unique and has its own needs and personality. Feng Shui is not a magic formula, but it provides us with tools and principles that we can adapt and apply according to the individual characteristics of our pets. Let's observe, listen and adapt our training techniques to ensure an enriching and harmonious experience for both us and them.

In conclusion, the art of Feng Shui provides us with valuable tips and techniques to improve the training of our pets. From the incorporation of natural elements and aromatherapy, to the practice of a coherent routine and non-verbal communication, every detail contributes to creating a balanced and stimulating environment for learning. In the end, harmony and deep relationship with our pets are at our fingertips thanks to the wonderful world of Feng Shui. Keep exploring these techniques and enjoy the training process with an energetic and loving outlook.

CHAPTER 15: Feng Shui in choosing the right food

We will learn how to use Feng Shui to select the most suitable food for our pets, promoting their health and well-being through nutrition.

Feeding our pets is a fundamental aspect of ensuring their health and happiness. But what role does Feng Shui play in choosing the right food? As we explore this fascinating connection between ancient Chinese art and our beloved pets, we'll discover how energy and balance can influence their well-being through their diet.

Feng Shui teaches us to harmonize our spaces to promote the flow of positive energy, and this also applies to the choice of food we provide to our furry companions. Like us, they are also energetic beings and are therefore affected by the same Feng Shui principles.

First of all, it is essential to consider the quality of the ingredients in the food we offer to our pets. By choosing a balanced and nutritious diet, we are providing them with the right support for their development and overall well-being. Following the principles of Feng Shui, we must look for high quality foods, made with natural and fresh ingredients, free of chemical additives and artificial preservatives. These quality foods provide a solid foundation for keeping our pets in optimal health.

In addition to the quality of the ingredients, it's also important to consider the way the food is prepared and served. According to Feng Shui, the presentation and aesthetics of food are key aspects to harmonize the energy that surrounds our pets during their meal.

Remember that the food must be presented on a clean and attractive plate, with an orderly arrangement that invites to the meal. Avoid old, worn or broken containers, as this can generate negative energy at the time of feeding.

Another aspect to consider is the location of the feeding area. According to the principles of Feng Shui, it is advisable to allocate a specific and quiet place for our pets to feed. This space should be away from loud noises, intense odors, and busy traffic areas. By creating a peaceful environment, we allow our pets to focus on their food and avoid distractions that can cause anxiety or stress during feeding.

Also, consider the orientation of the food area in relation to the layout of the rest of your home. According to Feng Shui, the location of the feeder and drinker should be in a balanced place, preferably away from narrow doors or corridors, and avoid them being directly in line with the main entrance. This helps to maintain harmony throughout the space and to avoid the interference of negative energies at the time of feeding.

As pet owners, it's our responsibility to ensure that our beloved furry companions receive the right food for their well-being. Feng Shui gives us a unique perspective to optimize this choice, taking into account both the quality of the ingredients and the creation of a favorable environment for their diet. By applying these principles, we are promoting the health and balance of our pets.

In the second part of this chapter, we'll delve even deeper into the role of Feng Shui in choosing the right food for your pets. We'll explore how the colors, materials and energy of food containers can affect the well-being and harmony of your furry companions. Get ready to discover techniques and practical tips that will help you create an ideal space for your pets to enjoy a diet in line with Feng Shui. Stay tuned, the best is yet to come. As we delve deeper into the fascinating world of Feng Shui applied to choosing the right food for our pets, we discover that there are several more aspects to consider. In addition to the basic principles that we have already explored, such as the quality of the ingredients and the presentation of the food, other elements such as the colors, materials and energy of food containers also play an important role in the well-being and harmony of our beloved pets.

One of the aspects to consider is the color of the food containers. According to Feng Shui, colors can influence the mood and energy of our furry companions. Each color has a particular vibration and energy, so it's important to choose the right color for our pets' food containers. For example, red is considered an auspicious color and can promote the good health and vitality of our furry friends. On the other hand, blue and green are colors that convey calm and relaxation, which can be beneficial during mealtime. Remember that the choice of color must also consider the preferences and personality of your pets.

The choice of material for food containers is also relevant to Feng Shui. Avoid plastic containers, as this material can contain toxic substances that can leach into the food and affect the health of our pets. Opt for stainless steel or ceramic containers, as long as they are free of toxic enamels or paints. These materials are safe, durable and easy to clean, promoting not only the health of our pets, but also greater durability in the containers.

In addition to considering the physical aspects of food containers, we must also pay attention to the energy that emanates from them. According to Feng Shui, food containers must be clean and free from any type of negative energy. It is advisable to clean food containers regularly, eliminating any food residue and stagnant energy that may accumulate. This not only ensures a healthier diet for our pets, but it also promotes a flow of positive energy into their environment.

Last but not least, it's essential to establish a consistent feeding routine for our pets. Feng Shui teaches us the importance of balance and regularity in all areas of our lives, and feeding our pets is no exception. Establishing regular meal times reinforces our furry friends' sense of security and stability, which in turn reduces stress and promotes their overall well-being.

Remember, as pet owners, we have a responsibility to provide the best possible care for our pets, and this includes choosing the right food and creating a favorable environment for their feeding. By applying Feng Shui principles to food choices, presentation and containers, we are promoting the health and balance of our beloved pets.

In short, we've learned that Feng Shui can be a powerful tool for selecting the right food for our pets. From the quality of the ingredients to the presentation of the food, the color and material of the containers, every aspect contributes to the energy and well-being of our dear furry companions. By paying attention to these details, we are creating an environment conducive to eating in tune with Feng Shui.

I hope this guide has provided you with valuable and practical information to optimize your pets' diet. Always remember to give them love, care and adequate nutrition, and you'll be amazed at the benefits that Feng Shui can bring to their lives. Keep an eye out for new ways to improve the health and well-being of your pets through this ancient Chinese art!

Chapter 16: The Importance of Water in the Home

We'll explore the importance of water in our home's energy balance and how to ensure that our pets have access to fresh, clean water at all times.

Water is an essential element in the life of all living beings, including our beloved pets. In the context of Feng Shui, water represents vital energy and symbolizes fluidity, purification and renewal. Therefore, ensuring that our pets have access to quality water is critical to their well-being and harmony in the home.

First of all, it's important to note that the water we provide to our pets must be fresh and clean. Like us, they need water that is free of impurities and harmful substances. In addition, the container in which they are supplied with water must be clean, avoiding any accumulation of bacteria or other elements that could affect their health.

Feng Shui teaches us that stagnant or dirty water can interrupt the energy flow in our home. This can have a negative impact on our pets and ourselves. For this reason, it is vital to maintain constant care for the water offered to them. We must change it regularly, making sure that it is always fresh and pure.

A great way to improve water quality for our pets is to use water filters. These devices are capable of removing impurities and providing healthier water. In addition, some filters also add minerals that are beneficial to the health of our pets. Remember that, just like us, they need to hydrate properly to maintain optimal body function.

Don't forget to consider the location of the water container. According to Feng Shui, water, being the element that represents fluidity and movement, must flow freely in the home. Therefore, if you have a water fountain, such as a small pond or decorative fountain, it would be ideal to place your pet's water container near this place. In this way, harmony and energy balance will be promoted in the environment.

Another aspect to consider is the amount of water we provide to our pets. We must ensure that they always have access to plenty of water, as dehydration can be detrimental to their health. In addition, in hot weather or during physical exercise, it is essential to increase the amount of water we supply to keep them properly hydrated.

In short, water plays a crucial role in the energy balance of our home and in the health of our pets. Providing them with fresh, clean water, in clean, strategically placed containers, is vital to maintaining energy harmony in the domestic environment.

In the second part of this chapter, we'll explore other aspects of water in the home that influence the well-being of our pets. We'll continue to talk about the importance of outdoor water spots, how to use fountains and waterfalls to improve energy in the home, and tips for harmonizing water containers and overall decor. Don't miss the next installment, where you'll discover more details about this fascinating topic. In the second part of this chapter, we will delve into other aspects of water in the home that also influence the well-being of our pets. We'll explore the importance of outdoor water spots, how to use fountains and waterfalls to improve energy in the home, and give you tips for harmonizing water containers and overall decor.

The presence of outdoor water spots in our home can have a significant impact on the energy balance and well-being of our pets. If you have the chance to create a pond or small fountain in your garden, you'll be providing a place of refreshing energy for your furry friends.

The sound and movement of water can be very relaxing and appealing to them, giving them a space to drink, cool off and play. In addition, these outdoor water spots can attract positive energy and ward off negative energy, creating a harmonious environment in the environment.

If you don't have the possibility to have an outdoor water spot, don't worry. You can use artificial fountains or waterfalls inside your home to generate a beneficial flow of energy. These fountains can be an attractive decorative element and, at the same time, provide fresh and stimulating water for your pets. Placing them in strategic locations, such as near a window or in a corner of the room, will allow water to flow and distribute positive energy throughout the space.

To further harmonize your pets' water containers with your home decor, it's important to carefully select materials and colors. Opt for ceramic or stainless steel containers, as these materials are safer and more durable. Avoid plastic containers, as they can contain substances that are toxic to the health of your pets. In addition, choose colors that integrate with the ambiance of your home. For example, if your house has a modern and minimalist decor, you can opt for water containers in neutral or metallic tones.

Remember that your pets' water containers are also part of your home's energy balance. Avoid placing them in messy or dirty places, as this can affect the harmony of the space. The ideal is to always keep the containers clean and in a stable location, away from drafts or high-traffic areas.

In addition to the aspects mentioned above, water can also be used as an element of energy balance in other aspects of decorating your home. For example, you can place images or paintings of waterscapes on the walls of your home to represent the fluid energy of the water. You can also use decorative elements such as fish tanks or table waterfalls to invoke the presence of water in different areas of your home.

In conclusion, in this chapter we have explored the importance of water in the energy balance of our home and how to ensure that our pets have access to fresh, clean water at all times. We have talked about the importance of keeping water in clean and strategically placed containers, as well as the possibility of creating outdoor water places or using fountains and waterfalls inside the home. We've also given you tips on how to harmonize water containers with your home decor. Remember that water is essential to the health and well-being of your pets, and its proper presence can have a positive effect on your entire home environment.

We hope you found this chapter useful and that you can apply these tips for the benefit of your beloved pets. In the next chapter, we'll delve into another key element of Feng Shui applied to your pets: the bedroom. You'll discover how to create a harmonious and peaceful space for your pets to enjoy a restful rest.

Chapter 17: The Art of Feng Shui in Choosing the Perfect Bed

We will find out how to select the perfect bed for our pets, taking into account the principles of Feng Shui and their individual needs.

In the wonderful world of pets, there's something magical about finding the perfect bed for our furry life partners. Just like us, our pets also need a comfortable and cozy place to rest and recharge. But did you know that the ancient art of Feng Shui can help us choose the perfect bed for them? In this chapter, we'll explore how to integrate Feng Shui principles into choosing the ideal bed for our adorable pets.

Feng Shui is an ancient oriental discipline that seeks to harmonize spaces with vital energy, known as Qi. Applying these principles to our pets' choice of bedding can provide them not only physical comfort, but also emotional well-being and energy balance.

The first step to finding the perfect bed is to observe our pet and understand their individual needs. Each animal has unique characteristics and preferences. For example, some dogs prefer to have a raised bed that allows them to have a panoramic view of the environment, while other cats enjoy closed beds that provide them with privacy and security. Observing their behavior and understanding their preferences will help us select the most appropriate type of bed.

Secondly, we must consider the size and shape of the bed. According to Feng Shui principles, a bed must be an appropriate size for the animal that will be using it. It is important that the bed is wide enough so that our pet can stretch and move comfortably, but not so big that it feels lost in it.

In addition to the size, the shape of the bed also plays an important role. According to Feng Shui, organic and curved shapes are more harmonious and create a sense of fluidity in space. Therefore, opting for rounded or soft-edged beds can be beneficial for our furry friends.

Another aspect to consider is the material of the bed. Just like us, pets can also be sensitive to certain materials or textures. It is advisable to choose beds with natural, breathable and easy to clean materials. This will not only ensure the comfort of our pets, but it will also promote the circulation of Qi in the environment.

Finally, we must not forget the location of the bed in space. Feng Shui teaches us that the position of objects influences the energy that flows around us. Placing our pets' bed in a strategic place, away from drafts and in a quiet area of the house, will give them greater calm and a sense of security.

As responsible owners, it's our duty to provide our pets with the best, and that includes choosing a bed that's right for them. By combining the principles of Feng Shui with the individual needs of our beloved pets, we can create a space where they can rest, relax and unleash their full potential.

Now that we've explored the importance of Feng Shui in choosing the perfect bed for our pets, it's time to dive into the practical details. In the second half of this chapter, we'll learn about the ideal colors and patterns for the bed, as well as the accessories we can add to further enhance your well-being. Read on to discover how to create a harmonious and loving environment for your furry companion. Now that we've explored the importance of Feng Shui in choosing the perfect bed for our pets, it's time to dive into the practical details. In this second half of the chapter, we will learn about the ideal colors and patterns for the bed, as well as the accessories we can add to further enhance the well-being of our beloved pets.

The color and patterns of the bed are also key aspects in the art of Feng Shui applied to our pets. Neutral colors such as earth and sand tones, as well as pastel tones, are the most recommended, as they convey a sense of calm and balance. Avoid colors that are too vibrant or strong, as they can cause excitement or agitation in your pet. Remember that the goal is to create a quiet and relaxing space for rest.

As for prints, choose soft and natural designs, such as floral prints or motifs inspired by nature. In addition to being aesthetically pleasing, these prints contribute to the feeling of harmony and connection with the natural environment, which favors the well-being of our pets.

In addition to the bed itself, there are accessories that we can add to further improve the rest experience for our pets. A popular option is to add extra pillows or cushions to provide additional support and comfort. These cushions can have soft textures or be filled with natural materials such as lavender or buckwheat, which can help calm and relax our pets.

It's also important to consider the location of the bed within our home. In Feng Shui, the location of objects within a space is considered to influence the energy that flows around them. Placing our pet's bed in a quiet area without drafts is essential so that they can rest uninterrupted. Avoid placing the bed near noisy appliances or in high-traffic areas, as this can cause stress or discomfort.

The environment surrounding our pet's bed is also important. Make sure you keep that area clean and free of clutter. This will not only promote a sense of harmony, but it will also make it easier to clean and maintain the bed.

It's essential to remember that every pet is unique, so they may need additional adjustments to their rest space. Watch your pet and be sure to pay attention to their individual needs. You can add toys or blankets that they like, or even create an additional relaxation area with a fountain of water or soft music. Remember that the ultimate goal is to provide a safe and welcoming space where your pet feels loved and protected.

In short, choosing the perfect bed for our pets is a process that goes beyond physical comfort. By incorporating Feng Shui principles, we can create a harmonious and balanced environment for our beloved furry companions. Careful observation of your individual needs, the selection of appropriate materials, calm colors and patterns, the arrangement of the environment and the addition of accessories can make all the difference in your overall well-being.

As responsible owners, we have the opportunity to improve the quality of life of our pets through small details such as choosing the right bed. Our pets provide us with unconditional love and companionship, and offering them a resting space that reflects our care and attention is one way to return that love to them. So, spare no effort in selecting the perfect bed for your adorable life partner, remember that they also deserve a special place to rest, dream and recharge.

Chapter 18: Feng Shui for Animal Communication

We will learn how to improve communication and connection with our pets through the practice of Feng Shui.

Communication between humans and animals can be a powerful and meaningful bond. Our pets are capable of providing us with unparalleled joy, love and loyal companionship. However, sometimes we can feel that there is a barrier between us and them. We wonder how we can strengthen that connection and communication with our beloved pets.

Feng Shui, an ancient Chinese philosophy, can be an invaluable tool in this process. The art of harmonizing the environment and creating positive energy flow can have a significant impact on our animal communication. By applying Feng Shui principles to our everyday lives, we can discover a deeper way to connect with our pets.

One of the key aspects of improving animal communication in the home is the balance of energy in space. Animals, like human beings, are very sensitive to the vibrations and energy of their environment. Therefore, it is important to consider the arrangement of the furniture, the colors of the walls and the quality of the air that surrounds our pets.

The first step in creating a harmonious environment at home is to pay attention to the arrangement of furniture. Think about how these are located in relation to where your pets spend most of their time. Are your pets' beds in a quiet and comfortable place? Is there enough space for them to move freely without obstacles? Make sure their seating area is cozy and gives them a sense of security and comfort.

In addition, colors also play an important role in the energy of a space. In Feng Shui, each color has a unique vibration and energy. For example, green is associated with harmony and health, while red can be stimulating. Look at the color of the walls of the rooms your pets are in and consider if these colors align with the type of energy you want for them. Soft, neutral colors can help create a calm and relaxing environment for your pets.

In addition to the arrangement of the furniture and the colors of the walls, it is also important to consider the air quality in the home. Make sure there is good ventilation and that spaces are clean and free of clutter. Fresh, clean air can help benefit your pets' overall health and well-being, which in turn can strengthen your communication with them.

Remember that Feng Shui is a continuous process and that every home is unique. You may need to make adjustments and experiment with different techniques to find what works best for you and your pets. As you move forward on your journey of improving animal communication through Feng Shui, you'll be opening the door to a world of deeper and more meaningful connection with your beloved pets.

Achieving more meaningful communication with our pets is a goal worth our time and effort. With the proper use of Feng Shui principles in our daily lives, we can open ourselves up to the possibility of a deeper connection. Next time, we'll explore practical techniques for applying Feng Shui specifically to animal communication. Keep reading to find out how to make the most of this wonderful practice in your relationship with your furry loved ones.

In this second half of the chapter, we will continue to explore practical techniques to improve animal communication through Feng Shui. Now that we've established the importance of energy balance in space and considered aspects such as furniture layout, wall colors and air quality, it's time to dive into deeper and more meaningful exercises.

A very effective practice for communicating with our pets at a deeper level is meditation. Meditation helps us to calm our minds, to focus and to increase our intuition. Sit in a quiet place in your home, preferably in an area where you and your pet feel comfortable. Close your eyes and breathe deeply, allowing your body and mind to completely relax. As you relax, imagine an energy connection between you and your pet. Feel how energy flows between you, how you intertwine and communicate at a deeper level.

Another technique you can try is creative visualization. Sit next to your pet and close your eyes. Visualize a beautiful green field, full of life and energy. Imagine that you and your pet are together in that field, enjoying nature and fresh air. Visualize how they communicate with each other, not through words, but through body language, energy and emotions. Allow yourself to feel the deep and loving connection that exists between you.

The use of crystals can also be beneficial to improve animal communication through Feng Shui. Place crystals such as rose quartz or amethyst in areas where you and your pet spend a lot of time together. These crystals emit positive energy and help to harmonize the environment, creating an atmosphere conducive to communication and connection with your pet.

Music can also play an important role in animal communication. Choose soft, relaxing melodies, such as classical music or specific music for pets, and set it in the background while you meet your pet. See how your pet reacts to music and how this can influence their mood and behavior. Music can help relax your pet and create a calm environment that is conducive to deeper communication.

In addition to these techniques, remember the importance of paying attention to the signs and expressions your pet shows you. Observe their body language, posture, and behavior. Learn to read the subtle clues and to respond accordingly. Animal communication is a two-way process, where you also play an important role in understanding and responding to your pet's needs.

In short, using Feng Shui in animal communication can open us up to a deeper and more meaningful connection with our pets. Through techniques such as meditation, creative visualization, the use of crystals and music, we can establish deeper communication with our furry loved ones. Remember that every pet is unique and may respond differently to these practices, so it's important to be patient and respect their individual needs.

I hope these techniques help you

Chapter 19: The Importance of Quality Time with Our Pets

We'll explore the importance of spending quality time with our pets and how to use Feng Shui to create an environment conducive to it.

The relationship we have with our pets is special and unique. They provide us with companionship, unconditional love and teach us valuable lessons about life. However, in our busy daily lives, we can sometimes overlook the importance of dedicating quality time to them. In this chapter, we'll dive into the relevance of this connection and how we can improve it through the practice of Feng Shui.

Our pets are sensitive beings that can perceive our emotions and energies. They need constant attention and often yearn to spend time with their owners to feel loved and safe. By dedicating quality time to them, we will not only strengthen our relationship with them, but we will also provide them with a balanced environment conducive to their well-being.

Feng Shui, an ancient Chinese system of harmonizing spaces, offers us tools to create an atmosphere in which our pets feel happy and in tune with their environment. By following some key principles of this practice, we can transform our home into an energetic haven for our beloved pets.

The first step in creating a supportive environment is to clear the mess. By freeing space from unnecessary or disorganized objects, we allow energy to flow freely and prevent the accumulation of negative energies. Our pets are highly sensitive to these vibrations, so a clear and tidy space will facilitate their relaxation and emotional well-being.

In addition, the proper placement of items in the home can also influence the energy that is radiated into the environment. According to Feng Shui principles, the location of food and water bowls, our pets' beds, and even the location of their toys, can have an impact on their physical and emotional well-being.

In addition, Feng Shui teaches us to incorporate natural elements into space. The presence of plants, for example, helps to purify the air and provides a feeling of vitality and freshness. In addition, choose soft colors

DISCLAIMER

The information provided in this book is for general informational and educational purposes only and is not intended as a substitute for professional advice, diagnosis, or treatment. The author and publisher have made every effort to ensure the accuracy and reliability of the information provided within these pages, but they make no guarantees, either express or implied, regarding the content's completeness, accuracy, or applicability.

Neither the author nor the publisher shall be held liable or responsible for any misunderstanding or misuse of the information contained in this book or for any loss, damage, or injury caused, or alleged to be caused, directly or indirectly by any treatment, action, or application of any advice discussed in this publication. The statements made within this book are not intended to diagnose, treat, cure, or prevent any disease. Readers should consult with a qualified healthcare provider for medical advice tailored to their personal circumstances.

The views and opinions expressed herein are those of the author alone and do not necessarily reflect the official policy or position of any agency or company. All content provided in this book is on an "as-is" basis and the author and publisher disclaim all responsibility for any errors or omissions.

Don't miss out!

Visit the website below and you can sign up to receive emails whenever Gonzalo Estrada publishes a new book. There's no charge and no obligation.

https://books2read.com/r/B-A-OZBBB-VFFZC

BOOKS 2 READ

Connecting independent readers to independent writers.

Also by Gonzalo Estrada

Self Healing
Visualiza tu Éxito
Cultivando Líderes
Afirmaciones y Empoderamiento
Semillas de Cambio
Cómo convertir TikTok en una máquina de hacer dinero
Cómo hacer dinero con Pinterest
Cómo hacer un ensayo
Cómo Pedir un Aumento de Sueldo
Currículo Poderoso
Entrenamiento sin Violencia
Entrevista Laboral
Gana Dinero con X (Twitter)
Ganar Masa Muscular
Volver a Empezar; el arte de reinventarse
Analiza Resuelve Ejecuta
Aromatherapy, The natural path to your pet's well being
Holistic Feeding
The ABC of educating your Pet
The Art of Cosmic Connection
The Art of Feng Shui applied to your Pets